I0021935

GOING IPAD

Making the iPad Your Only Computer

BRIAN SCHELL

Going iPad: Making the iPad Your Only Computer
Third Edition

Copyright 2019 by Brian Schell

Version Date: September, 2019

All rights reserved, including the right to reproduce this book or any portion of it in any form.

Written and designed by:
brian@brianschell.com

ISBN: 9781695170476

Printed in the United States of America

CONTENTS

INTRODUCTION

When experts and pundits use the phrase "post-PC," they are referring to being able to get real work done without using what we usually think of as a computer. The first time I remember hearing the phrase being commonly used was right after the iPhone came into existence, around twelve years ago. Although it has been possible for a rare group of people to dispose of their computers in exchange for a smartphone, that's simply never been a legitimate option for most of us. In my case, even if all the apps and capabilities were there, I'd never have the patience to look at that little phone screen all day long. No, a smartphone is not going to replace a full-size computer for most of us. Even if the software tools and capabilities are there, the form factor makes real work uncomfortable.

More recently, "post-PC" has been expanded to mean any computing or Internet device that isn't a regular PC. The lines are blurry and a little vague in many places. Many people consider a Chromebook a post-PC device, but other than a heavily locked-down operating system, is it any different from any other laptop? However fuzzy that logic may be, most people see a pretty clear distinction between computers and tablet computers. In 2010, the iPad was the first tablet device to really take off and be successful, and it's only grown in popularity. There *are* other tablet computers out there, but none have had the staying power or support of the iPad.

As I write this in late 2019, iOS 13 has just been released after being in the beta stages for months. Although iOS 12 wasn't really focused on new iPad features, this year's iPadOS 13 *is* a major iPad release; they even changed the name of the operating system from iOS to iPadOS. During this summer's WWDC event, Apple did an amazing demonstration of new multitasking, file handling, dark mode, sidecar, fonts, accessibility, and a bunch of new features and improvements in the new operating system. They once again emphasized the claim that more than ever, this would be the year you can replace your computer with an iPad. This also might be the first year that has actually been true for anyone other than writers. The newest iPad Pros are significantly faster than many of Apple's own budget laptops, so at least on the hardware side of things, this has been true since late 2018.

Prior to the release of iPadOS 13, some people have been able to use their iPads exclusively, but others are still having trouble making the leap to using the iPad with no computer. For many users, all the necessary tools are there, but for a few, mostly technical users such as coders, the tools still just aren't completely in place yet. Though with some compromises, this still may be possible. The purpose of this book is to help you decide which side of that line you fall on.

I skipped the first few iterations of the iPhone. I have always hated talking on the phone, and I didn't want the commitment of a two-year contract on the phone. The Apps weren't really a thing yet either. Back around 2009 or so, I gave in and bought an iPod Touch. It had games and apps without the ongoing expense of the smartphone. I'd played with them a bit at the store and thought the App Store was awesome. Over the next two years, I built up a nice little collection of games and apps for my iPod Touch, and then Steve Jobs introduced the iPad. From the beginning, I drooled over the pictures and images of this device that I hoped would be a "Super iPod Touch." When the device was finally released, critics lamented that "It's just a big iPod Touch!" Well, yeah– that's what a lot of us wanted– the iPhone ecosystem on a big-screen device. I was thrilled, and I've purchased almost every new iteration of the hardware since.

Just as a side note, I did eventually break down and join the "iPhone crowd" as well, starting with the iPhone 3GS. And as an another aside, the iPod Touch still exists and is a vastly underrated tool; it's essentially a "pocket iPad" for those who don't want an iPhone. We aren't going to be talking much about the iPod touch in this book, as it doesn't have some of the more advanced features of the iPad, but keep in mind that they still exist, and they are a nice addition to your arsenal.

As the years passed, new upgrades of iOS and improved generations of hardware came out, and we all wanted more. Power users wanted multitasking, better cloud access, improved syncing, and even file handling and USB support. And hey, why can't we use a mouse on this thing? The iPad has evolved to accommodate all those needs. In 2015, Apple released the first iPad Pro, a device that had a larger screen than any iOS device before it, and now allowed for easier use of a real keyboard or the new Apple Pencil. More importantly, Apple started an ad campaign that essentially stated you could replace your desktop with an iPad Pro.

This was true for some people. A select few writers, reporters, and people who used their iPad for very lightweight applications could, in fact, get most of their work done using the iPad Pro alone. Most people, on the other hand, still had one or two niggling reasons they still had to use a computer. Graphics processing, audio editing, coding and software development still have a few rough edges to work out and require some compromises. Getting data in and out of the iPad was often problematic as well, as iOS didn't support external drives or USB storage until *very* recently.

There's that word– compromise. That has been, and still is, the key to using the iPad as a main system. It's *not* a computer. It's not a laptop. It's not a desktop or phone. It's its own thing. It's the iPad, and it has its own way of doing things. You can't just throw away your laptop and switch to an iPad with no changes in the way you get stuff done. It's a different world, and in many ways, it's a *better* world, but you'll have to adapt some of your workflows as well.

Apple's iOS (now called iPadOS) and the app ecosystem have continued to evolve and get more powerful, and today, more and more people are making the switch to iPads. Sometimes they find some reason they still require a PC or Mac sitting at home or the office, but others actually manage to do *everything* on the tablet.

Just a final note that this book focuses on using the iPad, not IOS in general. Although most of the apps and procedures described here will also work on the iPhone (or iPod Touch), many of the interfaces and procedures are different, and I don't get into that here. If you're looking for guide to getting productivity-type things done on the iPad and iPad Pro, we're on the same page!

WHY DO THIS?

There are as many reasons to try to go iPad-only as there are users out there, but here are a few good reasons:

Cost - Say what you want about the iPad Pro being $800-

$1000, that still beats buying a MacBook Pro, and it's cheaper than many higher-end PCs. The iPad Pro isn't even needed for many people; a basic 9.7 inch iPad runs only $329 and is all many people need.

Safety - This is a big one. The Apple App Store is a closed ecosystem. You cannot install unchecked programs from unknown sources. Viruses and Trojans are essentially nonexistent. You don't need a virus scanner. Nothing is going to take control of your machine away from you. That's not to say all apps are amazing and wonderful; there are still some garbage apps on the App Store, but at least you don't have to be *afraid* to try out a new app.

Backups - The iPad backs itself up to iCloud automatically. You broke it? Someone stole it? You may be out the cost of replacing your device, but all your apps and data can be restored at the touch of a button.

Portability - It's thin, it's light, and it fits in a huge variety of cases. You can work pretty much anywhere using one. Going somewhere without Wi-Fi? You can even buy a version with 4G built in, just like a giant iPhone.

Minimalism - A lot of people do it just so they can say they have done it. Some people buy tiny houses, while others try to cut their possessions to a minimum. Back in the day, you had to have a tape recorder, camera, video camera, Walkman music player, DVD player, stereo system, type-writer, computer, and a bunch of other devices, but all of them can be replaced with a single device today.

Cost Savings for software Whether you prefer Mac or PC, most computer software is fairly expensive. $60 or more for a recent-release game is standard among console and computer gaming system. Office software can run a hundred dollars a year, and certain graphics packages require a costly subscription fee. On the other hand, most iPad apps are just a fraction of that. Of the hundreds of apps I've tried over the years, I can think of only three that I paid $20 for, while most are well under $10. Apps for the iPhone and iPad are just less expensive, even for pro-level apps. This isn't always a positive thing, as some makers of high-end, expensive computer apps won't go near the iPad due to low-price expectations among users.

I'm not going to spend chapter after chapter convincing you *why* you should want to switch (or try to switch) to the iPad-only lifestyle. If you've bought this book, I have to assume you're already interested, or at least considering, making the leap. Everything from here on out is going to explain HOW to do things, not necessarily WHY you'd want to do it— that's just assumed going forward.

BEFORE YOU BEGIN: PLANNING AND PURCHASING

There is a good bit of planning and preparation that must be done before you dump your computer. You can easily buy any app you need from the App Store, that's the beauty of the system, but your own data must be prepared a bit before you can rely on the iPad. You need to get your data into your iPad, and the easiest way to do that is to put it "in the cloud."

THE CLOUD

If you've done any kind of work with Apple devices in the past few years, you have at least heard of iCloud. That's Apple's own online storage system, which competes with Dropbox, Google Drive, Box, OneDrive, and many others. All these companies offer storage space on their own servers which are easily reached through the Internet. For most of your storage needs, it doesn't really matter which of these providers you use, but for most people, I would recommend just sticking with Apple's own iCloud service. It's built into all their devices, it's priced competitively, and it doesn't rely on advertising to pay for itself, so there is much less concern about privacy issues.

I've read dozens of articles over the years that complain that Apple's free tier, limited to 5 gigabytes, isn't enough space. They're right, it *isn't* enough for most people. Right now, before anything else, let me tell you that switching to the iPad isn't going to be *free*. You need to purchase the tablet itself. You need the apps, some of which will cost money. You may need some online services. And you will probably need to pay for some cloud storage space.

As of September 2019, here are the monthly rates for iCloud in the USA:

Cloud Space	Monthly Cost
5 GB	Free
50 GB	$0.99
200 GB	$2.99
2 TB	$9.99

Cloud Space vs. Monthly Cost

Five gigabytes is simply not enough to store most people's photo libraries alone, much less for backing up their devices. Let's just move past the idea that we need to skimp and cripple ourselves to save a dollar or three per month. When getting started, the 50 GB account *might* be enough for you, and that's probably where I would recommend you start unless you know right now you'll need more.

Actually, the 2 TB price is currently the same price as what Google Drive charges for half that much space, and roughly the same as what Dropbox costs. For once, Apple is actually cheaper than the competition!

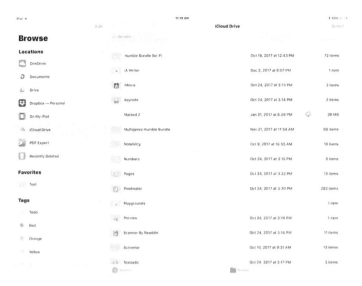

The Files app, with several cloud services displayed on the left

PHOTOS

Where will you choose to store your photos? This is actually an easy question to answer. Use whatever cloud-based system matches what kind of *phone* you have. If you have an iPhone, use the Apple Photo App. If you use an Android phone, you'll probably get more value from Google Drive and the Google Photos App. They are both excellent services, and whichever you pick, just be sure use it consistently. You can actually install both systems and have a double-backup of your pictures.

MUSIC

Again, there are options. Assuming you've moved away from audio CDs, most people have music libraries that are too large to simply load into the iPad in entirety, so again, a cloud solution is best. Apple itself offers two excellent music solutions for iOS devices: iTunes Match and Apple Music, and there are third-party offerings as well.

With iTunes Match, you load all your music into iTunes on a computer, which then gets "matched" with songs on Apple's servers and can then be streamed to your devices on demand. It uses very little storage space, and costs only $25 a year. It requires a lot of time to set up, especially if your music is all on CDs rather than encoded in MP3 files. One other point to consider is that if you get rid of your computer and really go iPad-only, you may have a really hard time adding new music to your iTunes Match library. A similar, competing service is Google Play Music, which lets you store fifty-thousand songs for free. It's not as well-integrated into iPadOS as iTunes Match, but it is an available choice.

Apple Music is a far simpler approach. It's simply an all-you-can-eat buffet of millions of songs, similar in features to Spotify or Amazon Music. These other services have iPad apps as well, so you can use whichever you prefer. No preparation or work is involved with these, just subscribe and start using it. Unlike iTunes Match, as Apple gets new music added to their collection, you get access to it instantly, with no effort on your part. Apple Music (or Spotify, Pandora, or Amazon Music) has a monthly fee, so it's a good idea to comparison-shop and take advantage of free trial offers to see which one you prefer. The service from Apple is integrated well with Siri, but otherwise, there's not much benefit over one of the competing services; go with the one you like best.

Also keep in mind that many users prefer to simply use their phone for music and not bother at all with music on their iPad. If you use AirPods or headphones all the time, that's a perfectly valid choice. On the other hand, the iPad Pro has excellent speakers, and there's no reason at all not to take advantage of them, especially if you already pay for some kind of streaming music service— Why not use it on your iPad as well?

DOCUMENTS

In this case, I mean non-media files such as word-processing documents, Excel sheets, PDF files, WAV files, and other materials in standard formats. These also get stored in iCloud Drive (or whatever cloud storage you prefer). If you have a large number of these, it may take a long time to get these sent to the cloud the first time. With the iPad Pro, you can also store and retrieve these files from a USB attached storage device, but the cloud is usually still simpler. We'll talk about this more later.

Again, for most of these uses, you don't have to use Apple products or services. I will mostly recommend the Apple products because they are usually better integrated into the operating system and are simpler to set up, it's easier to manage, you only get one bill each month, and most Apple solutions have built-in interactions with other apps, Siri, and Mac desktop computers (if you need them).

Apple Product/Service	Non-Apple Product/Service
iCloud	Google Drive, Dropbox, Box, OneDrive
iTunes Match	Google Play Music
Apple Music	Spotify, Amazon Music, Pandora
Apple Photo App	Google Photos

Apple Services vs. Similar Non-Apple Services

NO CLOUD? NO WAY!

Although the cloud is the best, most flexible solution for most people, you may want/need to do all your work on the iPad directly without using the cloud at all.

If this is the case, you have to get your data into the tablet the first time. There are two simple ways to do this.

The first, older method, involves using a cable to plug into your computer that runs the iTunes software (Mac or Windows) and then transfer all your data and files to the iPad from a computer. This is not difficult, but gets to be a hassle if you're constantly moving files back and forth between devices.

The newer iPadOS 13 method is to copy your files to an external hard drive or flash drive (using any needed dongles or adaptors), and then plug that storage device into the iPad and copy the files in using the Files app. It's the same process you would use to copy files to any "regular" computer.

If security is a major concern for you, then staying completely cloud-free may be a requirement. With the latest iPad Pros, there are configurations with as much as a terabyte of space, which is larger than many new laptops with SSD drives. Still, most people want the ability to synchronize files between their iPad and iPhone, or iPad and computer, or even multiple iPads. The easiest way to do this is through the cloud. Still, the cloud is *not* an absolute requirement. So if your job forbids you to use the cloud, you are not out of luck, but you may run into *some* limitations.

Apple has embraced cloud technology, and so have most other major computer companies. The cloud is not a fad, and it's not going away. Unless you have very specific security needs, just go with the cloud; life on the iPad will be much easier.

HARDWARE CHOICES

As I mentioned earlier, the iPad was introduced in 2010. Since then, there have been at least yearly upgrades and new versions, and there are quite a few different models you have to choose from. Although even the original model iPads still have some uses, many of the older models won't run the current versions of the operating system and therefore, aren't able to run the latest software.

Here is the list of iPad models that *can* support iPadOS 13 (As of September 2019; new models may be appearing in October):

- 12.9-inch iPad Pro (all generations)
- 11-inch iPad Pro (all generations)
- 10.5-inch iPad Pro (all generations)
- 9.7-inch iPad Pro (all generations)
- iPad (5th and 6th generation)
- iPad mini 4 and 5
- iPad Air (3rd generation)
- iPad Air 2

Any of these *can* work, but I tend to think the various **Pro** models are going to be the most useful for daily work. They allow the easy attachment of a keyboard, which we will cover in the next section, and they have the necessary processor power to run multiple apps at high speed. Keep in mind that they *all* run the same software, so they all *technically* can do the same things, but the form factor, speed, and screen quality do somewhat limit what is practical and comfortable.

ACCESSORIES: CASES

Apple itself makes several types of covers for the iPads, the smart cover, the smart folio, and the leather sleeve. There are literally hundreds, if not thousands, of third-party cases available.

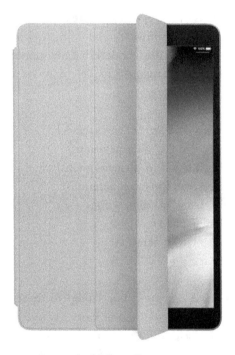

Apple's Smart Cover

Smart Cover The Smart cover is "smart" because when it closes, it uses a sensor to power off the screen. The smart cover magnetically attaches to the left side of the iPad and is just a cover for the front of the iPad; it doesn't protect the back in any way. It also can be very easily pulled off to allow access to the "naked" iPad.

Smart Folio

Smart Folio These look like the smart cover from the front, but also protect the back of the iPad from scratching. If you are going to use your iPad in a dirty environment or a place with "grit" that could scratch the back, this might be your best option.

Leather Sleeve These were introduced along with the 10.5" iPad Pro, and are just what they sound like. They're a leather sleeve that lets the iPad slip inside a slot at the top. These also have a little holder for the Apple Pencil.

Leather Sleeve

The trick here is in deciding how much you want to spend. The Smart Covers run $49-$95 and offer no protection at all for the rear of the iPad. The Smart Folio offers more protection, but also runs from $49-$129 The leather sleeve looks awesome, and does offer some protection, but Apple charges $129-$149 for them. This is one of those rare times when I recommend that buying a non-Apple product is the best choice. As long as it fits and offers the level of protection you need, why spend a bunch of money on an Apple-branded case? I have a nice faux-leather wraparound case that I bought for $14.99. Then again, if you aren't going to carry it around much, or **if you plan to get a keyboard that doubles as a cover**, you may not need a case at all.

ACCESSORIES: KEYBOARDS

Although you've always been able to use a Bluetooth keyboard with iPads, it's only with the introduction of the

Pro models that keyboards have really entered the main-stream for iPad use. The onscreen keyboard is still there, and sometimes when traveling it's the only way to go, but it's never been the most efficient option for typing a lot of information. If you plan to spend all day typing on the iPad, you're going to want to use a real keyboard. Here are the main options.

Smart Keyboard

Apple Smart Keyboard is Apple's foray into the world of keyboards. It attaches to the iPad Pro's smart connector. It folds away when you want to use the iPad as a regular tablet, and doubles as a cover when traveling. The keys themselves don't travel much, but they do feel good to click, and have a unique feel. It's a good choice, but it's not super heavy duty and are quite expensive.

Logitech Slim Folio Keyboard

Logitech Slim Folio Keyboard is one of many third-party keyboard cases, and is one of the better ones. The iPad slips inside a plastic case, which essentially turns the whole shebang into what looks like a laptop, and it's half the price of the Apple keyboard. It's got nice keys with good travel and a *real* keyboard feel. This is also one of the few iPad keyboard I've run across that has backlit keys.

Logitech K760 Solar Keyboard

Bluetooth Keyboards are an even more wide-open option. As I said earlier, *any* Bluetooth-capable keyboard can work with the iPad. If you go this route, you will probably need some kind of stand to hold up your iPad vertically like a monitor. I have used the Logitech K760 solar powered keyboard, and it works quite well, without the need to replace batteries... *ever*. One final option is to use a regular *USB wired* keyboard with the Camera Connection Kit that we'll talk about in the next section; I am typing this right now on a clicky mechanical keyboard from DasKeyboard plugged in with a wire. It's not as portable, but it sure is nice to type on.

ACCESSORY: APPLE PENCIL

Much has been written about the Apple Pencil since its intro-duction. It's light, charges quickly, and has the lowest latency of any drawing device I've ever come across. It's the closest thing to a real pencil available. Don't draw much? It still has uses:

• Doodling, painting, and art of all kinds

• User-interface controls. Dragging, moving and selecting can all be done with the pencil instead of your finger. I don't "draw" at all, as I don't even pretend to be an artist. Still, I use the Apple Pencil all the time while editing videos and podcasts on the iPad.

• Handwriting and notes

• Annotating and signing documents

ACCESSORIES: DONGLES AND ADAPTORS

The "Lightning to USB Camera Adaptor" is probably Apple's most poorly-named product. The version that supports SD Cards is certainly excellent for offloading photos from a camera memory card. The other one, the USB version, was created to directly connect a camera to the iPad for the same reason (offloading photos from the camera), but it can be used for so much more. It's a little dongle that allows you plug in any USB type A device into your iPad. There's also a similar USB-C to USB-A adaptor if you need to plug in an older device into the newer iPad Pros with USB type C.

Basically, whatever you want to plug in, Apple sells some kind of dongle or adaptor to make it work. There also are many third-party (non-Apple) companies that make accessories and adaptors. Many of these work perfectly, but some cheap knock-offs can actually be harmful to your equipment, so it's always *safer* in this case to pay a little more for the Apple stuff.

If you want to use your iPad Pro with an external monitor, you'll need the USB to HDMI (or USB to VGA) adaptors.

It's all pretty flexible: As I mentioned before, this book was all typed with a wired mechanical keyboard. This particular keyboard requires **two** USB-A ports, so I plugged both USBs into a small USB-C hub, and then connected the hub into the iPad Pro's USB-C port. This probably isn't something everyone would want to do, but it shows what is possible. I've also plugged in external USB microphones to do podcasting and audio book recording, and they work fine, although this probably hinges on the microphone's power consumption. Of course, flash drives and external hard drives will also work. It's just a matter of getting the adaptor that you need.

APPS: THE RIGHT TOOL FOR THE RIGHT JOB

The best indicator that the iPad is ready for prime-time work is that there are multiple apps available for almost any conceivable purpose. In each of the categories that follow, I list at least two excellent apps that can handle nearly any task. The hard part comes in choosing between some of them, as they are all excellent. Even so, new apps are added all the time, so always be on the lookout for new options.

OFFICE APPS

Microsoft Office

Whether you're coming from a Windows or a Mac environment, you probably have some experience with Microsoft Office. Although the entire Office suite isn't available (There's no Microsoft Publisher or Access, for example), Word, Excel, PowerPoint, OneNote, and Outlook are all here. All five work exceedingly well on the iPad, although they are somewhat more limited than their desktop counterparts. Still, you can load in and edit most documents without issue. Many features you might not expect to be included actually were, such as Tracking Changes, and they work perfectly. I've done editing and rewriting for clients, and they had no idea I was working from an iPad. Word, Excel, and PowerPoint (but not the others) require a subscription to Office365, which usually runs around $99 per year (or less with educational discounts).

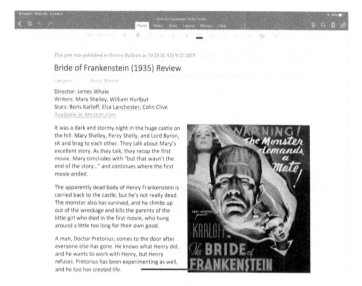

Microsoft Word

iWork Apple doesn't really promote "The iWork Suite" much any more, but the three main apps that comprise it, Pages, Numbers, and Keynote, are free to all iPad users and are some of Apple's best apps. These three apps are feature-similar to Word, Excel, and PowerPoint, but are created specifically for Apple products; hence they take advantage of Apple features more thoroughly. The main benefit of using these apps is that there is feature parity with the matching Mac apps. Anything you can do on your Mac will carry over to the iPad, and vice-versa.

Apple Pages, part of the iWork Suite

Google Docs As a third option, there is Google's office suite, Google Apps. Docs, Sheets, and Slides are the individual apps, and they are all tied together using the Google "file manager" app, Google Drive. There are some pretty major differences between these apps and the similar apps put out from Microsoft and Apple. For one, they are almost exclusively cloud-based. They are heavily tied into Google Drive rather than the more iPad-friendly iCloud service.

Google has been notoriously slow in adding new features to the individual Google Drive iPad apps. On the bright side, with the introduction of iPadOS 13, the Safari browser is now a desktop-class browser, and can run the web versions of the office suite. You can now forego the less-than-stellar iPad apps for Google Docs, Slides, and Sheets entirely.

Also, there is simply no equal in the realm of collaboration; if you work with others, this may be the best solution. Many schools use Chromebooks, and Chromebooks are heavily tied into this ecosystems as well. If that's an environment you need to accommodate, then this is the suite for you.

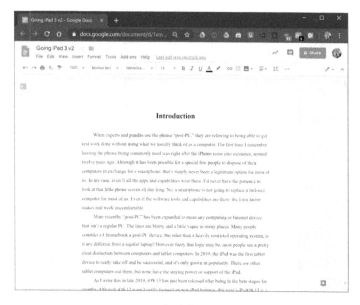

Google Docs

SPECIALIZED WRITING APPS

For most users, one of the above office suites is probably all that's needed for the task of writing, using either Word, Pages, or Docs. Some folks, on the other hand, need more precise control than a word processor can provide or are writing for special purposes. Here are three apps that look at writing in different ways:

Ulysses uses plain text files written in "Markdown" a simple way to describe text formatting that works very well for web publishing. Images, links, and formatting are all embedded directly within the text using simple tags. Ulysses goes a step further by incorporating everything you create into its own library system where everything is available to you without opening up files, saving, or anything like that. If you write for the web, or otherwise have reason to prefer Markdown, take a look at Ulysses.

Ulysses

Scrivener uses rich-text files to save your writing, but it specializes in long-form writing like books rather than short articles or business letters. Scrivener has special tools for research, and you can include research materials like PDFs, images, notes, and about anything else right inside your document workspace. It also has a flexible "compile" option that takes your finished document and creates nearly any kind of output you want, from Word document, to PDF, ePub, or about anything you need.

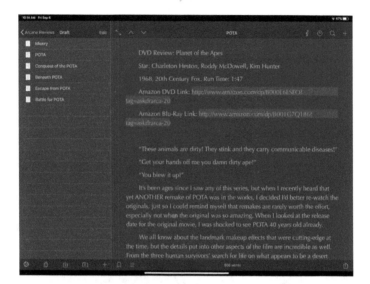

Scrivener

Textastic is a straightforward text editor. It has syntax highlighting for any number of programming languages, as well as for Markdown and LaTeX. It syncs to all the usual cloud providers, but also includes FTP, SFTP, and WebDAV file transfer. It includes a somewhat basic SSH terminal app as well, so if you work on a remote server, this might be the only app you need. It's also got a super neat cursor navigation wheel for quickly moving your cursor around the screen– this is a feature I wish more apps would implement.

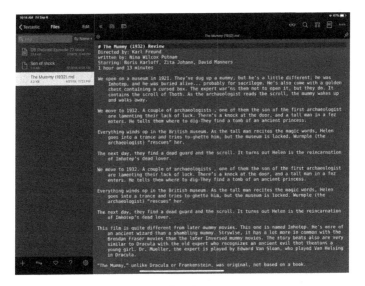

Textastic

TeX Writer uses a different kind of markup language called LaTeX. It's a fairly complex "language" that describes the text output you want and then compiles into a finished printable document or PDF file. It's more complex than either Ulysses' markdown or Scrivener's RTF-compiling, but is expandable and flexible enough to create literally anything on paper. It excels at math formulas and complex typesetting.

EMAIL APPS

Getting work done without email has become nearly inconceivable for most of us, so it's important to find just the right solution for you that works the way you work. Here are four of the most popular email app choices.

Apple Mail - This one comes included on all iOS devices, so you already have this one. It's not especially feature-rich, but it is reliable and easy to set up.

Outlook - This is Microsoft's email program for the iPad. It's similar to, but scaled down from, the desktop version. It still includes mail, to-dos, calendaring, and contacts, and most importantly, it syncs with the desktop version of Outlook, so if you use that at work, it's not much of a learning curve to get used to the iPad version

Spark or Airmail - I'm writing one entry for both apps because they are nearly identical in features and options. They are very different in how they approach these options, so I'd recommend trying both and making a decision. Both of them allow you to swipe right or left on the inbox to reply, delete, or archive the message. Both allow a lot of customization to their appearance.

I've tried all of these for long periods of time at some point, and my current email preference is plain old Apple Mail. Although Airmail and Spark add a lot of neat features, they would both, sooner or later, stop downloading my mail or wouldn't allow me to remove something from my inbox, or something equally annoying. Although a bit stripped-down, the Apple Mail app has *never* let me down.

DOCUMENT APPS

Before iOS 11 and the Files app came about, it was difficult to access and do work with various types of documents. Sure, you could load .doc files in Word, or text files in Textastic, but those tied a specific file format to a specific app. What if you wanted to be able to access/view/edit multiple types of files in a single app? That's where these come in. Of course, now you can load files into the location of your choosing in the Files app, but these apps still have their uses as a great way to organize your documents without dealing with file names and locations.

Documents is an app from Readdle. It allows you to

organize, download, upload, edit, or view dozens of different types of apps. It's such a "do-all" app that for many years, some people used it as THE 'filesystem' for iOS. If you have some need to download and carry data or documents with you *without* using the cloud, this is an excellent tool to use. Download the files to the app, put them in a folder for storage, and then access them when you need them.

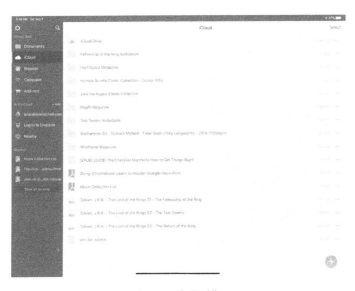

Documents by Readdle

PDF Expert is another app from Readdle. There are many PDF viewing apps out there, including the one from Adobe, but in my opinion, this is the one to have. It allows collection, sorting, editing, signing, filling in forms, and of course, printing. I recently sold our old house at long-distance and bought a new one, and the amount of paperwork and signatures were insane. PDF Expert came to the rescue several times with the ability to sign documents from another state with the Apple Pencil and email them in.

GoodReader was one of the very first apps available when the iPad first came out, and it's still a worthy tool. It's similar in function to Documents above, but also adds a variety of additional ways to get data in and out of the app including WebDAV, FTP, SFTP, AFP, and SMB servers.

Tip: GoodReader is excellent at listening to MP3-based Audiobooks that don't require a special app.

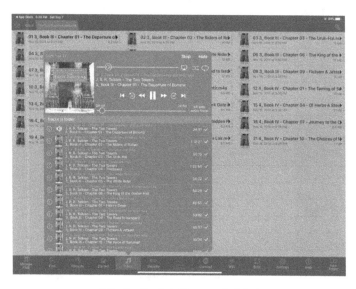

Using GoodReader to listen to an Audiobook

NOTE APPS

This is one of those areas where the iPad excels like no other device. All six of the apps listed here work awesomely, and they each have some feature that makes them outstanding. The hardest part of dealing with note-taking apps is sticking to only one.

Apple Notes The benefit here is that it's free, it's pretty simple, and it's already installed on all Apple products. It works with the Apple Pencil, and it's easy to insert images or text into a note. Still, it's a pretty bare-bones app for the most part.

Tip: If you touch the Apple Pencil to the "Lock Screen" of your iPad, the notes app will automatically load, allowing you to enter handwritten notes very quickly. This only works with Apple Notes.

Notability and GoodNotes These two are nearly identical in features, but operate in different ways. Notability allows you to work on a long, scrolling "endless page," while GoodNotes uses regular paper-sized pages where you turn the page to add more notes. Notability allows audio notes, so you can record while you write. GoodNotes allows easy text searching through your handwritten notes. They're both awesome, so maybe give them both a try to decide your favorite. The chief difference between the two is how you organize your notes: Notability has a sort of nested-list structure, while GoodNotes offers individual notebooks, that each have a cover of your own design.

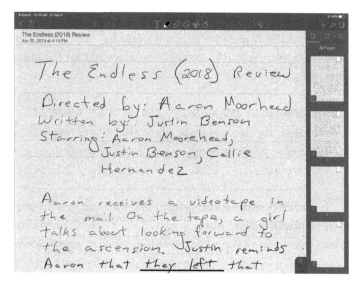

Notability

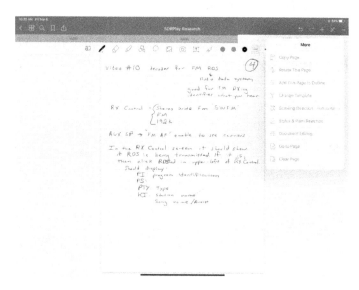

GoodNotes

Evernote This used to be the heavy-hitter in the note-taking arena. It's fast, reliable, and flexible, but they've raised their fees to the point where it's become a hard sell. Evernote is available on nearly every device made, so if you need syncing to non-Apple products, this may be the best choice.

OneNote is part of Microsoft Office, but unlike most of those apps, you don't need an Office365 subscription to use this. It's completely free, but does require that you set up a OneDrive account (also free) to store your notes. This is one of the better-looking note apps, with each "notebook" having a tabbed layout, where each tab can have multiple pages. There are a lot of options for sorting and filing your notes.

OneNote

Drafts This one is a little unique. It's not so much a note manager, but is designed to be a super-quick way to get text into your iPad (or even better on the iPhone). Click the icon, and a blank screen appears where you can instantly type.

There's no fooling around with files, pages, or notebooks, it's just a blank sheet for "text acquisition." I've found I use this one a lot on my Apple Watch. I can dictate into the watch, and the text appears inside the app on my iPad, where I can then cut and paste it into other apps.

> Tip: The dictation feature in Drafts doesn't have any kind of time limit, unlike Siri Dictation. If you want to dictate something longer than a few seconds, give Drafts a try.

SECURITY

One thing you don't generally have to worry about when using the iPad is viruses. Since everything installed on the iPad comes from Apple's "walled garden" of the App Store, there's no way you can catch a malicious virus on your system. That does not, however, mean you don't still have to be concerned about security. Two areas of concern worth look at are password security and WiFi sniffers.

1Password and **Lastpass** These two are password management systems. They each can generate and keep track of a database of thousands of web sites and passwords, and are especially useful in creating secure passwords. You can set up a "recipe" for passwords telling how many characters, punctuation symbols, or numbers you want to include, and it generates what you need, completely randomly.

Either of these apps are a great help. I've gone from weak passwords such as

```
USER: brianschell
PASSWORD: PENCIL (or the cat's name or my
```

```
birthday or something equally easy to
guess)
```

```
to
```

```
USER: brianschell
PASSWORD: zagw@JPTfVquVkQjvAetx2ZiA
```

Obviously, a password like that is hard, if not impossible, to remember. Or type for that matter. Fortunately, 1Password will copy the password into the clipboard for you, or in many cases enter the password in the login form for you automatically.

1Password keeps all your passwords and other secure data in an encrypted file on your device, where no one else has access to it, or it can sync via Dropbox or iCloud to your iPhone and/or computer. Lastpass, on the other hand, keeps the data on their servers, which keeps it synchronized on all your devices but therefore is a little less secure (in my opinion).

1Password is more expensive than Lastpass, but in my opinion is the better choice— *if* you only work on Apple or Windows systems. Lastpass works through the web browser and is compatible with pretty much *any* web-capable device, so that may make a difference for you.

1Password

VPN Software One of the primary benefits of working on the iPad is that you can go anywhere to get work done. The local coffee shop or burger joint is as good a place to work as the library or your home office. Anywhere there is WiFi available can become your office (or literally *anywhere* if you can tether with your phone or buy an 4G compatible iPad). One problem using public WiFi systems is that they aren't really secure. Even if they claim that they are safe and secure, how do you *really* know?

One way to be sure is to be proactive about it. If you use a VPN (virtual private network), all your network data is encrypted as it leaves your device, and it stays that way until it hits the destination site. This way, even if someone along the way "intercepts" your network data, they have no way of reading it. It's actually *very easy* to set up a packet sniffer, so if you use a lot of public WiFi, this is a must-have item.

There are dozens of VPN companies out there, each

selling their own solutions. Some claim to be free, but I'd strongly recommend you stay away from them. I use a company/App called NordVPN. I don't know if they're the best choice in the world, but I've been happy with their reliability, and they have apps for most every system available. I use ExpressVPN on iOS, MacOS, Windows, Linux, and even my Chromebook (Yes, I have a lot of tech).

Here's a screenshot of the NordVPN app open. It's using a server in Ukraine. Why? Because I've never been there and it sounds exotic.

Nord VPN linked to a server in the Ukraine

What's the point of this? Any website that tries to detect your location now thinks I'm in Ukraine. In the next screenshot, I'm going to Google Maps to see where it thinks I am:

Google Maps thinks I'm in Ukraine!

This gives web apps that track your location, like Netflix and Amazon, a huge headache.

BROWSERS

Which web browser you choose is largely a matter of choice and what you've gotten used to in the non-iPad world. Although Safari wasn't much better than the others prior to iPadOS, now there's a very good reason to choose it over the others.

Safari has gotten a lot better with this version. It's now a full desktop-class browser, which means it can run all the major web apps, such as Google Docs, Squarespace, and YouTube. All work the same on the iPad as they do on any regular computer. Apps like Google Docs, that used to require a half-baked app to run, now run natively in Safari. Apple's browser also has a "read it later" feature that is quite nice, as well as tabbed browsing. It also tends to be faster than the competition most of the time.

Chrome is probably the most full-featured browser out there, with the most compatibility with the web. Most sites "just work" without issue on Chrome.

Firefox has been all but forgotten until recently. With their new 'Quantum' version for the desktop (and presumably soon for iPadOS), they are making something of a comeback. It has integration with Pocket, one of the major read-it-later services, and has a very powerful screen-shot and screen-saving system.

iCab This one is a good choice for privacy-oriented users. As I said a moment ago, Safari now runs as a desktop browser, but iCab has the ability to "disguise" itself as any other browser on the market.

COMMUNICATIONS

Messages is Apple's iMessage app. It can text back and forth with other users of Apple products. If you have an iPhone, this is the default messaging program for SMS. It has a lot of interesting features (maybe too many features, in my opinion), such as stickers, iMessage apps, sound effects, and image search.

Slack is a major communications platform for many small businesses. You can set up custom "chatrooms" for groups and departments, and all communications can be kept in one place.

Telegram is similar to Slack. Which one you choose depends on what your friends or colleagues use (possibly both).

Facebook Messenger the app for Facebook used to have the messaging built-in, but a while back they split the messaging functions off into its own app. If you talk to Facebook friends privately, then you'll need this app.

IRC has been around for decades, and is still going. This text-based chat system allows you to connect to many specialized servers, not just one centralized company, so it's a very robust system. IRC isn't an app, it's a server protocol. If you want to *use* IRC, then an app like **Igloo IRC** or **LimeChat** is needed.

FaceTime, Google Hangouts, and Skype are good if typing, texting, and emailing aren't your thing, and you'd rather just *call* someone. That's an option too. The iPad is not a convenient replacement for your phone, but it's right there in front of you all day long, so *why not* use it for calls? These three apps each offer voice-only or face-to-face video calling. Which do you want? That depends on your clients or whoever you're calling. None of the three are intercompatible, so you need to have what the person on the other end is using. Note that *Google Hangouts* is scheduled to be shut down and discontinued in late 2019, so by the time you read this, it may be already gone.

Google Voice is yet another option, and this one allows you to send and receive phone calls to or from people with real telephones, regardless of what kind of system they are using. Google Voice is, however, audio-only. All of these solutions are free within the USA, and inexpensive for worldwide "long-distance" calls.

SOCIAL MEDIA

Although it's completely possible to do all your social media activity on your phone, sometimes it's nice to be able to use the big screen of the iPad. Actually, social media is the *primary* use of the iPad for many people.

Facebook is still the king of all social media sites. You have a choice in how to access it on the iPad: either via the Facebook App or through Safari or some other web browser. The Facebook app simplifies things quite a bit, and it also hides many of the ads. The web browser version is, of course, the full experience, including all the ads. It just depends on how you prefer to work.

Twitter, like Facebook, can be run through a browser or an app, but it offers a vast number of choices in apps. **Twitterific**, **Tweetbot**, and many others offer many more features and a better interface than the default app from Twitter itself.

Tweetbot Twitter Client

Instagram isn't like the others. Instagram (so far) has never released a version of their app for the iPad. Their app is available on the phone, and meant for the phone, as they want things to remain completely mobile. You can still install it on the iPad, and it works. But it looks somewhat stretched, doesn't fill the screen, and doesn't offer any special features. There are other, third-party, apps available for *browsing* Instagram, but Instagram doesn't allow these apps to upload photos. There's a section later in this book about how to download iPhone apps like Instagram instead of iPad apps.

Reddit has quickly become one of the busiest and most influential sites on the net. Whatever your interest, there's probably a subreddit for that. Although there is an official Reddit app, there are some excellent third-party apps, including **Narwhal** and **Apollo**. I personally use the Reddit App on my iPhone and Narwhal on the iPad. Be warned though, once you start on Reddit, you can easily get hooked.

GRAPHICS, ART, AND PHOTOS

Apple Photos is the default photo application that comes with all Apple products. It's a nice way to store your photos in the cloud and sync between all your devices. It's reliable, simple, and has just enough editing ability to fill most regular people's needs. If you aren't a graphic designer or professional photographer, then take a good hard look at this one. It does most of what non-graphics professionals need.

Affinity Photo if Apple Photos won't cut it for you, then this is the "Big One" for the iPad. Dedicated retouching tools, non-destructive adjustments, super-accurate selections, liquefying effects, real time effects, realistic brushes, advanced layer support, works with RAW and EXIF data, tone mapping, 360-degree images, focus merging, and a lot more. It's the most "Pro" app available right now.

Lightroom and Photoshop from Adobe are the kings of photography in the computer world, but their offerings are somewhat limited on the iPad. Although these two apps are available (as part of their subscription service) they are scaled-down and feature limited compared to their desktop versions. If you're already buying the Adobe service, then by all means give these a try, but do your research about specific needs if you plan to rely on the Adobe offerings. If you aren't locked into the Adobe ecosystem already, I'd recommending looking at similar, non-subscription apps first.

Pixelmator is another app that works brilliantly for basic photo manipulation and touch-ups. I use this one to design the covers for my books. It handles layers, text, graphics, photos, and most everything else I've needed. I am not a graphic designer, so it must be relatively easy to learn. If you want "something like Photoshop" but don't want to subscribe to the Adobe service, this is where you should start looking.

Pixelmator and the book cover

Others There are hundreds of fun, and often free, photo manipulation tools out there. They can automatically fine-tune your colors, add filters, do silly special effects, create collages, do face-swaps, and all kinds of other neat things.

Many of these apps are designed for the iPhone, but keep in mind that you can load iPhone-only apps onto your iPad as well.

Google Photos If you use an Android phone instead of an iPhone, this is probably a must-have. Essentially this is Google's version of Apple Photos. It uploads and syncs your photos with basic image editing features. It's free, so it's worth looking into. One thing that many people do is to install this app, and then set it up to upload all images from the Apple photo app to Google. This allows for what is essentially a free backup for all your photos.

Procreate and the Author's Awful Mugging

ProCreate is just one of many "painting" apps out there that take advantage of the Apple Pencil. Most of the apps I've mentioned do allow for some drawing or painting features, but they are all mostly organized and designed around editing photographs. ProCreate and similar apps are meant for taking a blank canvas and creating art from scratch. Some use more of a painting metaphor, while others are more like a sketchpad or watercolor set. There are dozens of these kinds of apps out there, and they all have strengths. If you're an artist, you'll want to try several, and probably pick a few that you switch back and forth with. My two favorites are ProCreate and ArtRage, although if you're an artist, you'll find dozens of apps that entice you.

AUDIO EDITING

Twisted Wave is an audio editor. If you do any kind of audio editing, for audio books, radio shows, music, or podcast production, this is an awesome app to check out. You can do noise reduction, cut-copy-paste, fade-in and fade-out, and lots of other effects and tools for making your voice sound good. Twisted Wave is about as close to the desktop computer software Audacity as you can currently find on the iPad.

GarageBand is an audio editor as well, but unlike Twisted Wave, this one is more focused on musicians. It has dozens on built-in instruments, midi sequencing, and includes smart instruments. It's a powerful app that does many things well up to a point. You may find that your needs are more than it can handle, but if you need quick (and free) tools for audio, look here first.

Ferrite is an app geared toward podcasters and those interested in creating and editing short spoken-word recordings. It has numerous sound-enhancing effects, allows for multi-track recording, and works well with longer audio files. I regularly create and edit hour-long podcasts a hundred percent of the way through all the steps from recording to uploading a file with complete metadata and show notes, all from within Ferrite.

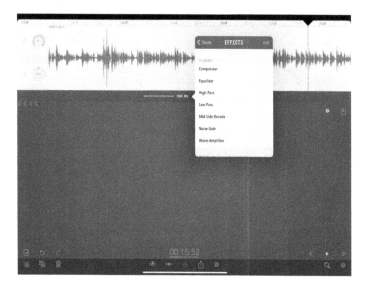

Editing a Podcast with Ferrite

Auria is a full-fledged digital audio workstation for recording and arranging multi-track audio. It covers all the bases- recording, mixing, and post-production. It handles up to 24 tracks and supports a huge variety of plug-ins and enhancements. If you mix music, you have to take a look at Auria.

Tip: For spoken word recording, go with ferrite. For recording live music, try Auria.

MUSIC, GAMES, AND ENTERTAINMENT

Games may be the single-largest category of apps for the iPad. Many, many people buy an iPad just for the gaming options. And the games are excellent. I'm partial to strategy games like **Dominations** and **Civilization VI** on my pad. There's far too many options and choices to get into much detail here; iPad gaming could be a book unto itself. You know what kind of games you like, don't be afraid to install them all. Lots of them are free, and even those that aren't will often give you a taste before you buy the full version.

Tip: A new feature of iPadOS this year is the ability to connect an Xbox or PS/4 Dual-Shock controller to your iPad through Bluetooth. The game has to support the controller, but as time passes, more and more games should take advantage of this.

Music Apps are extremely popular on both the iPhone and iPad. With the enhanced speakers on the iPad Pro or the ease-of-use and quality of Apple's Airpods, the iPad is a wonderful audio platform. We looked at **Apple Music** in the section on the Cloud, but that is only one of many popular music services available for the iPad:

• Apple Music
• Spotify
• Amazon Prime Music
• Pandora
• Google Play
• TuneIn

All of these are great, and there's no reason you need to limit yourself to just one. TuneIn and Pandora have excellent free services, and if you are signed up for Amazon Prime, you have (limited) access to their music service free with that. The two big players here are Apple Music and Spotify, and both have good features and similar pricing; you'll want to take advantage of the free trial offered by each to compare and decide.

Apple Podcast App is the simplest way to get started

listening to podcasts. You can do an easy search for podcasts titles and episodes, easily subscribe, and it works with both audio and video podcasts. It doesn't offer the features of Overcast, but it's free and already included on your device. If you enjoy podcasts, I need to recommend two: **Adapt**, a show all about iPad, and **AppStories**, a mostly-Mac show that often discusses iPad topics.

Overcast Podcast Player

Overcast is the premier app for listening to podcasts. It has an easy search function, good download and archival functions, the ability to download or stream shows, and a lot more features that Apple's podcast app doesn't offer. One of the most popular features of Overcast is the "smart speed mode." This automatically detects blank spaces and longer-than-needed pauses between words and removes them. This can often take a one-hour podcast and drop it down to fifty minutes. Nothing at all is lost, and you saved ten minutes. If that's not enough, there's also a feature that can play the podcast at whatever speed you want, from around ninety percent of the original speed to three-hundred percent. Listen to more stuff in less time. It is limited, however, to audio podcasts— It doesn't do videos.

Netflix is a video streaming services that is immensely popular, and an excellent value. If you already get Netflix through some other device, you should download the app and try it on your iPad.

Amazon Prime is another video streaming service. It's included with an Amazon Prime subscription, so if you already have that, try the video streaming. The selection of shows isn't anywhere near what Netflix has, but they do have lots of good stuff and original content not available anywhere else.

Hulu is another video streaming service. They, too, have shows that the two previous services don't, so it's are worth a look too.

TV Networks HBO, History Channel, Discovery, NBC, ABC, CBS, PBS, BBC, Crackle, A&E, and most other networks have their own apps. Some require a subscription, some require you to have a specific cable package, and some offer a selection of free shows. If you have a favorite show or network, it's worthwhile to try their app and see what deal they offer.

BOOKS, COMICS, AND READING APPS

There's nothing that matches going on an overnight trip and having an entire library in your hand. You can buy specialized e-reader devices like the Kindle, Nook, or Kobo Reader, among others. These are nice, small devices, and some have e-ink, which is *very* easy on the eyes to read. These are great devices, but each one is locked into their manufacturer's own ecosystems. With the iPad, you can access **all** of them. Load in the specific apps for Kindle, Barnes & Noble, or Kobo, and then you have access to all the books you've bought from those companies.

Apple Books (formerly iBooks) is the e-book software from Apple. I don't think I've ever actually *bought* a book from the iTunes store, but it's my reader-of-choice for DRM-free books that I get elsewhere. I often buy book bundles from http://HumbleBundle.com, and those books are easily loaded into Books.

Kindle, from Amazon, has been around a long time, and they control a huge percentage of the ebook market. There's a good chance you're actually reading this on a Kindle (I won't judge!). Still, you don't **need** to own a Kindle *device* to read Kindle *books*. You can simply download the app from the iTunes store, put in your Amazon credentials, and then download all your books onto your iPad. I have an older Kindle device, and I've bought tons of Kindle books, but I usually end up reading them on my iPad because it's always with me.

Apple News is an app with a subscription service ($9.99 per month as of September 2019) that gives you unlimited access to dozens of full-color monthly magazines in multiple genres. These are the full book, even including the ads. If you get many paper magazines in the mail, you should look at this. By canceling just one or two paper magazine subscriptions, you could pay for the Apple News subscription and get loads of included books every month. These aren't just junk, either, they're big-name magazines. People, Sports Illustrated, National Geographic, The New Yorker, just to name a few.

Comic Books are huge on the iPad. The device itself is about the same size as a comic book, and it offers full color, so it's nearly the perfect way to read comic books. **Comixology**, **Marvel Unlimited**, and **Dark Horse**

Comics all have readers that tie in with their respective services, while **iComic** and **Comic Flow** support loading comics from any source.

NEWS AND WEATHER

News isn't exactly entertainment, but it works similarly to the TV Network apps above. Whether you like USA Today, The BBC, FOX, CNN, or something local, there are probably specific apps that carry the news. Depending on how you like your news, there are videos, web-based newspapers, podcasts, radio streaming, and, of course, social media. It's very easy to get overwhelmed with *too many* news sources, especially if you have notifications turned on. Apple News, mentioned above in the section about magazines, also has a selection of newspapers and websites that can be read through the app.

Stocks was a new app with iOS 12, but has been around since the early days of the iPhone. If you follow the stock market or financial news, give this one a shot.

Weather Forecasting is one area where the iPad really shines. There are many great weather apps, all being updated continuously.

Weather is Apple's stock weather app. It's got Siri integration, which is nice, but it's pretty bare-bones in features and doesn't have much detail. I recommend using something else.

Weatherbug has long been my favorite weather app. The large, full-screen interactive maps with pinch-to-zoom features are fun and really useful when there's a storm that might or might not hit you.

Weather Live by Apalon is a beautiful weather app with nice maps, easy to find forecasts, and overall is just pretty to look at.

TASK MANAGERS

There are as many ways to keep track of tasks and to-do lists are there are people. Whether you just need a simple list or are a strict "Getting Things Done" adherent, there are tools for your needs. You can easily use any of the "notebook" apps that I discussed earlier to keep track of your to-do list, but if you want something with more options that is devoted to nothing but task management and/or scheduling, here are the best options.

Reminders has been heavily updated this year, with a bunch of new features. You can now add not only tasks, but sub-tasks, to allow for individual steps in larger projects. You can include attachments such as images, documents, scans, and web links to a task, which makes it faster to find related materials. You can set up recurring events, and even reminders based on your location. The primary draw for this one is that it has the best Siri integration. You can just say, "Hey Siri, add 'take out the trash' to my reminders list" or just "Hey Siri, when I get home remind me to take out the trash." If you're looking for something to take advantage of Siri, this is a good one.

Todoist, Wunderlist, and Things are three of the big to-do list competitors. Todoist and Wunderlist have free options, while Things is a one-time purchase. All three do basically the same thing in three different ways, so you should check them all out to see which one works better for you. Todoist is my preference, simply because it works every-where– Apple, Android, Mac, Windows, Chrome, or the Web. I bought the premium version for a year once and really didn't even need those features, so the free edition may very well be all that you need. It is for me.

Tip: I've recommended the free level of service from

Todoist for several years, but this year, I'm going with Apple Reminders. It does almost al the same stuff, and it works better with Siri, so the switch is a no-brainer for me.

OmniFocus is the "pro level" of task management and calendaring. If you live and die by your planner, if you have meetings around the clock, this may be what you need. With versions from $30 to $60, it's the most expensive of the tools here, but if you need the best, this is the one, although it's probably more than most people need.

Trello is nice way to organize big projects. It's a *Kanban board*, or something like a whiteboard full of Post-its that you can rearrange. It's a great visual way of organizing, rearranging, and assigning tasks, either just for yourself or in collaboration with others.

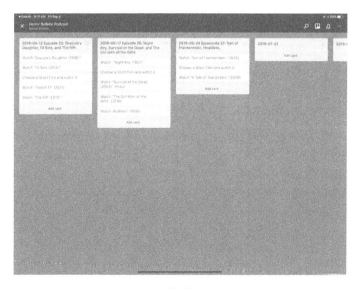

Trello

Apple Calendar is installed on every iPad by default,

and it's a nice, basic calendar. It has the benefit of Siri integration, so you can simply say out loud, "Hey Siri, add 'take a nap' to my calendar for today at one o'clock," and it will do it. On the negative side, Apple Calendar hasn't seen any significant upgrades in years, and many third-party apps have features that leave this one wanting more.

Google Calendar has similar features to Apple Calendar, but has easy synchronization with Google's calendar service. If your school or company uses Google services, this is probably the first app you should look at for calendar work.

Fantastical is an enhanced calendaring app. Although it offers many customization and automation features that Apple's calendar doesn't have, the primary selling point of Fantastical is that it allows you to add events and reminders using natural language. It reduces clicking and scrolling, just allowing you to type in "set a reminder to take out the trash for every Tuesday at seven-thirty." It will parse that sentence, understand it, and set up the calendar and reminders appropriately. It's pretty smart!

CODING / PROGRAMMING / WEB DESIGN

Coding, whether it be something as detailed and low-level as compiled C or as straightforward as HTML, is not something that everyone needs to worry about. But if that's what you do, then you probably spend a LOT of time using the tools. First, I should point out that with the exception of Pythonista (mentioned below), there aren't any full-featured compilers or interpreters available on the iPad; you'll probably want to edit files locally and FTP or SSH (or something similar) to a remote server to actually implement your work.

Textastic (again) Back in the section for writing apps, I mentioned the Textastic text editor, and it's still my favorite text editor for coding work too. It has ftp/sftp/webDAV transfers and SSH terminal built in as well as the usual cloud integration, so getting your work in and out is easy. It also works well with Working Copy and Github.

Working Copy is a full-featured Git client for iPad (and iPhone). With Working Copy, you can clone repositories, view and edit files, commit changes, and push commits back to the server. You can use other applications to open files inside Working Copy, letting you edit images, text files or even SVGs in the editor of your choice.

Code Editor (Formerly Coda by Panic Software) is another text editor with file management features and syntax highlighting. Upload and download via ftp easily, and edit the files using the text editor, graphic editor, or whatever you need right on your iPad.

Code Editor by Panic

Pythonista is, to my knowledge, the only full-featured programming environment available on the iPad that comes complete with a compiler. It's a complete development environment for writing Python scripts on your iPad. Lots of examples are included — from games and animations to plotting, image manipulation, custom user interfaces, and automation scripts.

In addition to the powerful standard library, Pythonista provides extensive support for interacting with native iOS features, like contacts, reminders, photos, location data, and more. If you want to do programming on the iPad and actually *run* the code on the iPad, this is the app to check out.

Shortcuts (formerly Workflow) isn't *exactly* a coding app, but it's certainly the first place to go for any kind of iPad automation or "scripting." You can build an automation "script" by dragging and dropping little code blocks around and choosing from each object's options and properties. It sounds a little simplistic, but it's *very* powerful once you have learned the basics.

Shortcuts (formerly Workflow)

Termius and/or **Blink** are two easy-to-set-up SSH clients. Use them to connect to your remote command line system and run apps in a full-screen shell. These two both have added the use of MOSH, so they never disconnect. You can run your terminal all day long, even on "iffy" Internet connections. Using an SSH app greatly increases the range of power-user options available to you. My other book, "Going

Command Line" delves into this option in great detail, check it out if this is an option that interests you.

SSH into a Raspberry Pi with Blink Shell

Cloud Solutions are another option. All the above are apps that you install on your iPad. Some edit files locally, others remote into some distant server, but they're all apps. Another option is to use a cloud-based editor. Examples of these would be **CodeAnywhere** at https://www. codeanywhere.com/ or **Cloud9** at https://aws. amazon.com/cloud9/

TEAM-UP: USING THE IPAD ALONG WITH A COMPUTER

So far, we've been working under the assumption that you are working *only* with the iPad. That's a legitimate choice, but that is an artificial requirement; you probably **do** have a regular computer sitting around somewhere that you could make use of if there was a good reason. The iPad is great on its own, but if you sometimes *need* a PC or Mac app, then you aren't out of luck. Here's a couple of nice ways to make use of the old PC or Mac *in addition to* the iPad.

Screens VNC is a VNC — *Virtual Network Computer*. It lets you connect to a computer (PC, Mac, or even Linux) and control it from anywhere, not just from within your home. Use your screen as a big trackpad and control the computer's cursor with your finger. Tapping or double-tapping the screen translates to left- or right-clicking. I've found that it's a little too laggy for gaming, but for "normal" work, it's great.

SSH/MOSH is another method of doing remote work.

Back under the "coding" section, I mentioned the apps **Termius** and **Blink**. These allow you to connect to a remote terminal server and type in commands into a text window. That may sound positively prehistoric to many people, but there's a *lot* of power in a command line, and some people work that way exclusively. See my book, "Going Text: Mastering the Power of the Command Line" for a real life-style change. Another benefit of this is that you can "rent" or subscribe to a service that offers servers very inexpensively, so you don't even need to own or set up a computer for this.

Google Chrome Remote is from Google, and has the benefit of being completely free, so there's no reason not to try it. Just install the Chrome Remote Desktop app from the Chrome Web Store on your computer (Mac, PC, or Linux) and the app on your iOS device (iPad or iPhone). You set up the connection, and then see your computer's desktop on your iPad. Move your finger around on the screen, and the on-screen mouse follows it. Tap to click. Run your computer apps, transfer files, whatever you want to do. If you have files at home on your PC and need them while you're working remotely, you can "Remote" into your computer and retrieve them.

Sidecar is a new feature that turns your iPad into an advanced second display for your Mac computer running MacOS Catalina. You can move your mouse off the right edge of your Mac monitor and see it appear on the left edge of the iPad and keep going. There's no lag as you have the option of using a wire or doing it wirelessly. Plus, it adds the benefits of a touch screen, so you can use your fingers or the Apple

Pencil to tap, zoom, and so forth on your Mac apps through your iPad screen.

Apple Sidecar

Astropad isn't like the others above. Instead of taking over the computer and running apps, this one turns your iPad into a graphics tablet similar to those sold by Wacom. You use your iPad and Apple Pencil to draw on your iPad, but your movements and work are sent through Bluetooth to the Mac. This means that you can essentially run the computer version of Photoshop, Pixelmator, Affinity, or any other computer graphics program and control it from your iPad. Although this is possible with Screens or Chrome Remote Desktop up to a point, Astropad is geared solely toward graphics/pencil performance. If you are an artist, and need the full computer version of your chosen art program, you should look into this one. This one only works with Macs, not PCs.

WEB APPS

Everything up to this point has either been included on your iPad for free or is easily available for download from the App Store. But the App Store isn't your only option. There are also countless web-applications available over the Internet for free or for a subscription fee. Some people survive just fine using nothing but a Chromebook as their primary computer, and, until recently, they used nothing *but* web applications... and we're looking at them in this book as almost an afterthought.

Many web-based apps didn't work properly on earlier versions of Safari, as the browser identified itself as a "mobile device" and could only download the limited "phone version" of many websites. This year, Safari has finally gotten serious with its browser and made it a full desktop-class browser, able to load the full version of most web sites. If you tried some kind of web service before and didn't like the experience, it's time to try again— You may get better results.

Word, Excel, and PowerPoint - I mentioned these apps

earlier and said they required an Office365 subscription to run. That's true enough for the *apps*, but they also exist as Web-browser apps that you can use for free online. The web-apps are somewhat more limited than the App Store versions, but they may be enough for your needs.

Overleaf - I mentioned the app TeX Writer earlier in the book as a tool for writing in LaTeX on your iPad. Another option is to use the Overleaf.com website. It's a free service (if you don't need collaboration), that lets you write, edit, and preview LaTeX documents "in the cloud." The original text and paperback version of this book was written and designed completely on the Overleaf site.

Gmail is the world's most popular e-mail service, and it's completely compatible with all the email clients I mentioned earlier, but many people still prefer to just use the Gmail.com website to access their mail.

Google Apps (aka Google Docs and/or GSuite) is one of the most popular cloud-based systems for getting work done. There's Google Docs, Sheets, Slides, and a handful of other apps. They're the best apps going to collaborative writing, and millions of students and businesses use these apps exclusively. These used to require clunky, poorly-made apps from the app store to run, but with iPadOS, they now work just fine in Safari, as do all the apps mentioned above.

This book isn't going to focus too heavily on web-apps, as I cover them extensively in my other book, "Going Chromebook: Living in the Cloud," and really only intend to cover *iPad-specific* tools here. Just keep in mind that if you can't find a tool you need in the App Store, there may be a tool on the web for your needs.

GETTING WORK DONE

And that wraps up our overview of the various apps and tools that are available to you in the iPad world. New things are being introduced and updated all the time, so keep an eye on new apps in the App Store. Now we move forward on some of the ways to use these things.

Safari's Download Manager

Safari isn't new by any means, but this year Apple has added several major new features. We've already talked about how Safari now identifies as a desktop-class browser, able to load Google Docs, Squarespace, and many other web-apps. Another big improvement is that now Safari has a download manager built in.

Open up Safari and browse to a web site that allows you download a file. In the following screenshot, I have clicked to download a ZIP file containing a bunch of audio files:

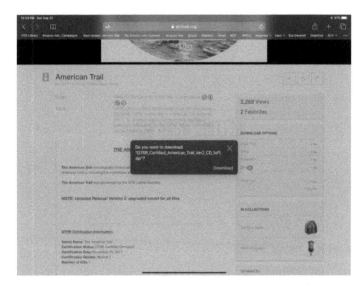

Verifying that we want to download this file

Since I do want to download the file, I tap on "Download." Up in the top right-hand corner is an icon for the download manager:

Download Manager

Note that this icon doesn't appear until you have started a download. Then there is a small progress bar under the icon that shows the download progressive's of the file. Once the file is completely downloaded, you can click on the icon to see the file:

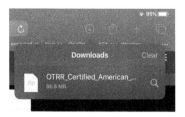

A File in the Download Manager

If you click on the magnifying glass icon, the Files App will load and show you the downloaded files on your iPad. From here you can copy, move, open, or do whatever it is you want to do with the file. In this case, I chose to download a ZIP file which contains other files, so if I click on the file's icon, it will create a folder and "unzip" those files into the new folder, which I then can access individually.

DARK MODE

New in iPadOS 13 is the long-awaited Dark Mode interface. Well, it was long-awaited by *me* anyway. This switches most apps from a dark-text-on-light-background to a light-text-on-dark-background. This makes things generally easier on the eyes in low-light environments, as you don't have nearly so much bright white glare from the screen.

I've always been a big fan of dark themes and dark modes, and most of the screen shots in this book were done with the apps in dark mode. To switch between Light and Dark modes, go to Settings and tap on "Display & Brightness." The first option at the top of the screen allows you to choose between the two, or even set it to automatic, where you can set a specific schedule or change themes depending on whether the sun is up or down.

USING A MOUSE

It's taken thirteen versions of the operating system, but it's finally possible to use a mouse with your iPad. Still, using the mouse isn't the same on the iPad as it is on a desktop computer, so some adaptation is going to be necessary.

You can use either Bluetooth or wired mice, but at this time, there are some limitations concerning which mice you can use. For example, my (expensive) *Apple Magic Mouse 2* that came with my iMac doesn't work on my iPad Pro, but the $3 generic wired mouse that I picked up at a flea market ten years ago works fine. This is a new feature, so it should only get better with time.

To set up your wired mouse, plug it in using a dongle or adaptor if necessary. I had to use a USB-A to USB-C adaptor to plug it into my big iPad Pro, but otherwise, there was no special trick to it. With a Bluetooth mouse, set your mouse to pairing mode and pair it with the iPad in the same way you would pair any other Bluetooth device (Settings->Bluetooth->Connect). If it won't pair, try turning your iPad all the way off and back on again. This does help sometimes.

Assuming you were able to get your mouse to pair or is plugged in, go to the Settings app and click on "Accessibility" and then click on "Touch," which results in the screen below:

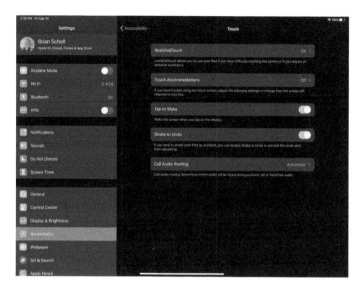

Accessibility > Touch

Once you get to this screen, you can click on "Assistive Touch" to see the following menu:

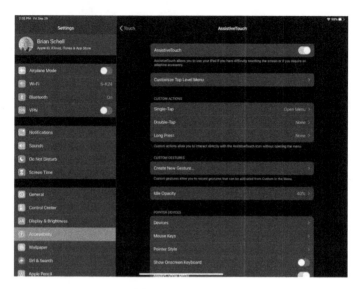

Accessibility -> Touch -> Assistive Touch

Once Assistive Touch is on, on the same screen is an option for "Devices." Under the Devices menu, you should see whatever connected or paired mouse is available:

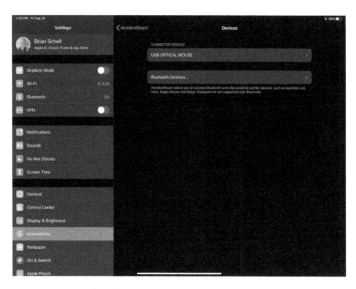

Choose the Pointing Device to use as a mouse pointer

Again, if your device doesn't work, don't be too surprised, this is a very new feature. If your mouse shows up on the list, click it, and you should be good to go. In my screen shot above, I chose "USB OPTICAL MOUSE."

The mouse pointer appears as a round circle instead of the arrow used every other device, but it's essentially an avatar for your finger. Click on a place and move up to swipe up for example. Anything you can do with your finger, you should be able to do with this pointer.

Also, by default, once AssistiveTouch is turned on, the "AssistiveTouch Menu" (the little circle located somewhere on the right-side of the screen) is turned on by default. I have found this annoying, and if you right-click the mouse, this menu comes up by default, so it really isn't necessary. You can turn this off from within the AssistiveTouch menu under the option "Always Show Menu." Turn this off to make the little circle go away.

KEYBOARD AND VOICE INPUTS

On-screen typing has improved since the iPad was introduced, and the on-screen keyboard has been updated and improved a number of times, but it's still made of glass, and it still doesn't offer any kind of touch-typing feedback. Some people have learned to make it work for them, so I won't say it can't be done, but I've found that typing on glass is less efficient than a "real" keyboard. I'm not alone in this, which is why people made such a fuss when the iPad Pro was built with a keyboard in mind. That said, iPadOS 13 has added some new features related to the onscreen keyboard:

QuickPath is a feature that Android devices have had forever, but has been very slow in coming to iOS. You can "swipe" your finger from letter to letter on the keyboard without raising your finger from the glass. To type the word "swipe," for example, you put your finger down on the S then slide over to the W then to the I, and P, and E. Then you raise your finger off the keyboard and "swipe" appears. It's a little strange getting used to it, but it can be a lot faster than typing each letter one at a time. This is good on the iPad, but it really stands out on the smaller iPhone screen.

Floating Keyboard is another new feature. "Pinch" on the keyboard to make it smaller, and then you can drag it around to various locations on the screen. It's often easier to thumb-type in the middle of the screen than down at the bottom where the keyboard usually pops up, and now you have a choice! Note that you *can* combine these new features. Drag the floating keyboard to the edge of the screen and then use your thumb to swipe around and type using QuickPath.

Keyboards have already been discussed in the hardware section, so I won't get into it again here other than to remind you that you don't have to use Apple branded keyboards.

Literally any Bluetooth keyboard will work, as will most wired keyboards with the camera connection adapter.

Keyboard Shortcuts

Using a physical keyboard has additional benefits beyond just faster typing:

• Holding down the Command key will pop up a screen showing all keyboard shortcuts for the current app.

• Command-Tab brings up the task switcher, allowing you to switch back and forth between currently running apps without touching the screen.

• Command-Space brings up Spotlight, which has a lot more functionality than it appears at first glance. You can search for anything here: installed apps, data files and documents, and even stuff on the web. You can type in your search immediately without clicking on anything. Hit command-space and just start typing. It's very efficient. Type the first few letters of an app name, hit Return, and the app starts. The same goes with specific non-app files or web sites. It's fast! If you search for an app and see an icon for the app, you can drag it down to the left or right side of the screen for split-screen use.

The following are "standard" keyboard shortcuts that should work for editing text in most apps:

• Command + A: Select all text
• Command + X: Cut
• Command + V: Paste
• Command + Z: Undo
• Command + Shift + Z: Redo
• Option + Left: Move cursor one word to the left
• Option + Right: Move cursor one word to the right
• Option + Shift + Left arrow: Select previous word
• Option + Shift + Right arrow: Select next word

Voice Dictation is often overlooked. With this option enabled, just press the "microphone key" on the on-screen keyboard and start talking. You'll see your text entered as you speak. It's great for short emails, text messages, and notes, but it is limited in how long you can talk– it times out after about thirty seconds. For the ability to speak for longer periods and to add more features, look to Nuance Software's Dragon Anywhere for more professional narration features for a premium price (it's $15 a month).

SIRI

This has come up a few times under other topics, but Siri itself is quite useful on the iPad. Just say, "Hey Siri," and Siri will ask you what you want. Then you just speak simple commands to it. Sometimes it works, sometimes it fails with hilarious results, but once you get used to it, it's quite useful.

Siri has a great deal of integration with the various Apple apps such as Apple Music, Reminders, Calendar, email, messages, and many more. The list of commands is huge, and it's being constantly added to. Quite often, your phrasing has to be exact or in the correct order for Siri to understand you. Here is a recent list of all commands to try out: https://www.digitaltrends.com/mobile/best-siri-commands/

The recent addition of Siri Shortcuts in iOS 12 makes Siri far more useful and customizable than it's ever been. You can record your own commands and link them to sequences of actions that make voice control much more useful. At the time of this writing, Siri Shortcuts is still improving as of 2019, as many new tools as options have been added this year, but there's still plenty of room for improvement.

IPHONE APPS

Almost all the apps we've discussed are designed for the iPad itself. There are some very good apps available that are designed only for the iPhone, and these also work on the iPad. They often look stretched out, but they are functional. Instagram is one case that was mentioned; they don't support iPad, but their iPhone app works just fine.

You're almost always going want to use the actual iPad version of an app if there is one, but if you want an iPhone app instead, here's what you do:

Looking for iPhone Apps on the iPad Store

1. Go to the App Store.
2. Click on the magnifying glass to search for an app.
3. Type in the name of the app.
4. Assuming there is no iPad version, you won't find the thing you're looking for.

5. Up in the top-left-hand corner of the screen, click on "Filter."

6. The first choice on the list is "Supports" and next to that is "iPad Only." Click that and choose "iPhone Only," and different results will appear. If there is an iPhone version, you can choose that and download it normally.

7. The next time you do a search, the store will automatically revert back to looking for iPad software.

MULTITASKING

For most of the iPad's existence, we had to make do loading in one app at a time and switching between them by double-clicking the button. All apps were full-screen, and multitasking was limited at best. Things have changed. With iOS 11, things improved significantly, and then iPadOS 13 added several additional improvements. Split-view multitasking, drag and drop, and other enhancements make it a lot easier to run more than one app at the same time and move data between apps easily.

SPLIT VIEW

Split view is done most easily by dragging an app's icon from the dock at the bottom of the screen to either the right or left side of the screen and releasing it. This little "floating" window is called the "slide over" view. You can "lock in" an app into split-view mode by dragging the title bar downwards just a little bit until it spreads out to fill the side of the screen or dismiss the floating window by dragging it off to the right. If you have dismissed the floating window (by dragging it off the right-hand side of the screen), you can bring it back by swiping left from the right edge– reversing what you did before.

You can then adjust the width somewhat by dragging the middle divider line, located between the two apps, to the left or right. If you have two apps side-by-side and need a third app, you can have the third app in a slide-over floating window over the first two apps. Drag the app you want to open from Dock over the Split View slider (the divider in the middle of the screen) and drop it. Now you have **three** apps open on the screen and running at the same time.

MULTITASKING

Once you know how to set up the split-screen apps, the rest is pretty easy. The system works best with two apps, side by side, or three if you count the slide-over view. If you need to bring in yet another app just drag it up from the dock and drop it over the app on the left or the right to replace it. The app will then be replaced onscreen with the new app. The old app hasn't stopped, you just can't see it.

For more complex tasks, or for running more than two apps at once, you can switch between running apps using a keyboard by hitting Command-Tab. This brings up a task switcher that should be pretty easy to use; just press Command-Tab repeatedly until the app you want is selected.

You can also switch between apps in slide-over mode by swiping left or right on the little bar at the bottom of the slide over window as shown below:

Switch apps by sliding left or right on the slide-over bar

DRAG AND DROP

Assuming both apps support drag and drop, moving information from one side of the screen to the other is as easy as
sliding an icon or item to the other app. This is something
you're going to need to experiment with to get the hang of it.
Apple has put a lot of work into making drag and drop intelli-
gent and intuitive.

IPAD VS IPHONE

Remember: You don't have to make your iPad mirror your
iPhone. It's OK to leave your music and social media on the
phone and leave your iPad for "real work." Actually, you
might be a lot more productive if you did just that, but it's
your device– make it work for you.

WIDGETS

Another tool to get your work organized that is often under-utilized is the widget screen. Widgets now appear on the home screen instead of a separate screen in previous versions of iOS. Mine looks like this:

Widgets on the left side of the Home Screen

To set up your widgets, scroll to the bottom of this screen and choose "edit." Use the red "-" buttons to remove the apps that you don't use, and then click the green "+" buttons to add those that you do.

Keep in mind that there's just so much space on the screen before you have to start scrolling, so put the ones you will use most at the top. You can have a ridiculous number of widgets on the widget list if you choose, but I've found that I *never* actually scroll down on this list, so anything more than what you see in the picture is pretty much useless.

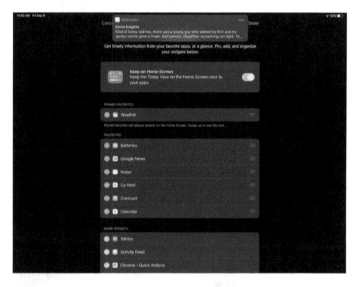

Adding and Removing Widgets

Going back to the screenshot of my widgets again, I start with the Weather widget. I often use the Apple Pencil and Apple AirPods, and their battery status shows up in the Battery widget. Then you can see I have Google News and Apple Notes showing me a recent note.

The widgets are a nice time-saver if you get in the habit of using them; a lot of people never bother at all, so it's certainly not a "must-use" feature. To tell the truth, I rarely use them on my iPad, but they are very handy on my phone.

FONTS

Apple includes a wide variety of very good fonts, but some-times you need something more. If you have a TrueType font from your computer or downloaded from the web (these files end in .ttf), you can install it onto your app using the **AnyFont app**. Once installed, you should be able to use the font in Apple Pages, Microsoft Word, and most other apps that allow you to switch fonts.

AnyFont

SHELF APPS

Shelf Apps work by sitting on one side of your screen, in either Slide Over or Split View, and then acts as a temporary shelf where you can place files. Some of the most popular shelf apps as of this writing are **Gladys**, **Dropped** and **Yoink**. The one I use is called **Yoink.** I like it because it works with many different data types:

- Locations from the Maps app
- Emails from the Mail app
- Images
- URLs (with rich previews)
- App links
- Attributed text

• Plain text

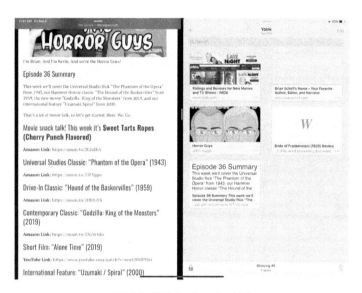

Yoink Shelf/Clipboard App (on right)

You just drag (or cut and paste) files into Yoink, and leave them there until you need them. Things that you have put in Yoink stay there until they are removed, unlike a computer clipboard that goes away when the system is rebooted.

REMOTE WORK

I mentioned using SSH to remote into a server in the coding section, and you can get a lot of powerful work done that way, but working on the command line isn't for everyone. Sometimes you need the power of a "real" computer **and** the mobility of your iPad. You actually can do both!

Screens VNC is an app that allows you to access your Windows PC or Mac computer from your iPad. Assuming your computer is fairly recent and you have a fast Internet connection, lagging can be minimal and response time is often very good. You can run literally any app on your computer and control it through your iPad from anywhere. About the only major limitation I've found is that you get no audio from the computer. That kills most games, and doesn't allow for audio editing either. Still, it's highly useful for anything textual or for accessing things quickly.

PRINTING FROM THE IPAD

First things first: The iPad will only print to AirPrint-compatible printers. If your printer needs to plug in with a wire, it won't work. It *might* be possible to plug an old, wired printer into a regular computer and share it somehow, but that's beyond the scope of this book. I'm going to assume you have a supported printer.

You'll need to follow the printer's instructions to set it up to connect to your network, add a network password, and so forth. Most printers include fairly simple step-by-step instructions to get going. Getting the printer working on your network is going to be the hard part; getting the iPad to print is actually really simple.

Printing from the Share Sheet

Assuming the printer is properly set-up, the iPad will pretty much detect everything and do its own set-up. For some apps, like Apple Pages, just choose the clearly-marked "Print" option and follow the on-screen instructions.

Most apps don't have a simple menu option marked "Print." They require you to use the "share sheet." That's the little icon, usually in the upper-right-hand corner, that shows a square with an arrow coming out of it. Most apps have this somewhere. Click that and then choose "Print." You may need to scroll the list of the options to the right or click on "More" to enable the printing option to show.

At this stage, you should be presented with a dialog asking about which printer you want to use, how many copies, and perhaps other options. If you don't see a printer here, check the settings on the printer itself.

IMAGE AND DOCUMENT SCANNING

Back in the day, you needed a flatbed scanner to read in papers that you wanted to keep electronically. Today, you just take a photo of the paper(s), and software will detect the edges, adjust it for any misalignment, and even join multiple pages together as a big PDF. It's easy and surprisingly high-quality.

Sometimes, the Apple Notes app is all you need for this, and other times you may want a dedicated scanning app.

Scanner Pro by Readdle is a great one, allowing you to send your scanned documents to multiple cloud services. Another nice option is **Scannable** by Evernote, which does the same thing but uploads the resulting file to the Evernote system and OCRs the page into their database for easy searching.

Also there is a new feature in iPadOS 13 that allows you to scan documents directly from the Files App. Open the Files App and navigate to some location where you'd like to save a document. Then click the three-dots button (...) above the "Browse" list. One of those options is "Scan Documents," and if you click on this, the camera will allow you to photograph a document and crop/trim extraneous information out of the image. It's really useful!

HOMEKIT

This is an area I can't go into much detail on, as new products are becoming available nearly daily. Once you have some kind of HomeKit-enabled device, such as lights, locks, thermostats, or something else, make sure it's properly assembled and turned on.

1. Open the Home app and tap "Add Accessory" or tap the "Plus" icon.

2. When your accessory appears, tap it. If asked to "Add Accessory to Network," tap "Allow."

3. With the camera on your iOS device (it might be easier with an iPhone), scan the eight-digit HomeKit code, or QR code on the accessory or accessory documentation.

4. Add information about your accessory. Siri will identify your accessory by the name you give it and the location it's in.

5. Tap Next, then tap Done.

APP ORGANIZATION

The iPad is a mixed bag when it comes to flexibility. You have a lot of options when it comes to organizing your files and icons on the home screen and dock, but it's not unlimited flexibility. The icons on the home screen are limited to five rows of six columns each, and you can have fifteen icons on the dock. These are maximums. You can combine your apps in folders, and these are limited to sixteen apps per screen, although you can have multiple screens in a folder.

One choice you probably need to make early on is whether you are going to use folders or not. You can have your apps all out on the "desktop" and simply let them flow over into multiple screens, not worrying about the folders. This is certainly the simplest way to go, and if you don't have many apps, probably the best method.

Another method is to have all your apps on one screen, but sorting them into relevant folders. Folders are easy to create. Just hold down on any icon until it starts "wobbling" and then drag it on top of another icon. A folder will be created with both icons inside it, and you'll be prompted for a name for the folder.

I've included a screen shot of my own home screen above for your consideration. I'm not saying my way is best, but I use the iPad a lot, so it works for me:

Author's Homescreen

First, notice the background. It's black and blue. I like bright colors, but after a long day of looking at the screen, it makes me crazy. A dark, less-distracting background seems to help, and I almost always use the new dark mode as well. At least that's my preference. I have all my most commonly-used apps on the dock:

- Omnifocus [Task Manager]
  - Textastic [Text Files]
  - Dominations [VERY addictive Game]
  - 1Password [Password Manager]
  - Files
  - Calendar
  - Safari
  - Apple Notes
  - Narwhal [Reddit Client]

- Ulysses [Writing App]
- Apple Photos
- Documents [Media organizer and player]
- Apple Mail
- Settings App
- Chrome Browser
- Three most recently-used apps [Shortcuts, Screens, and the App Store in this case]

So you can see that I'm not exactly locked into Apple Apps only. There's a hefty dose of Google and Microsoft stuff mixed throughout. I've tried **a lot** of apps, and I've chosen the ones that work best for me, regardless of who makes it. Again, that's just my way of doing things, but there is a lot to be said for choosing one ecosystem and going "all in" with it.

Outside of the dock, I have "second-tier" apps that I use regularly, but rarely alongside other apps. Because of the way multitasking works, I've found it easier to put the apps I often multitask with in the dock; it makes it easier to drag them up later.

You can't see them in the screenshot, but my second screen (swipe left), are my "Other" apps, all loaded into folders. I have one for Utilities, Social Media, Entertainment, Games, and Apple Junk. "Apple Junk" isn't saying those aren't great apps. They're apps I never use, but at the same time, I don't want to delete them (or can't delete them), so they have to go somewhere. I don't usually have any "bare" apps on the second screen, just folders containing apps.

GESTURES

Swiping and pinch to zoom are common enough features on most devices that I'm not going to get into those here, but there are some less-than-intuitive gestures that I'm going to point out now.

Swipe up from bottom of screen and release = Shows the Home Screen (same is clicking the Home button)

Swipe up from bottom of screen and hold for a moment = Shows the App Switcher, with all open apps on one screen, making it easy to switch between running apps. This is the same as double-clicking the Home button if you have an older device with a button.

Task Switcher

Another way to do something similar with a keyboard is to hold down the CMD key while pressing TAB. You can hit TAB repeatedly to switch between running apps.

Keyboard-Based App Switcher

Swipe down from the upper-right (i.e. touch the wifi/battery area and drag down) = Shows the Control Center, with many quick settings available to you. These buttons can all be customized from within the Settings App.

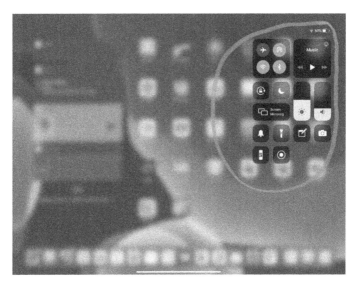

Control Center

Swipe up from the bottom just a little and hold = brings up the Dock.

Hold down on the on-screen keyboard's spacebar = Turns on "Trackpad Mode" where you can move your finger around the keyboard and the cursor moves like it would with a trackpad. This is a little tricky to master, but invaluable if you do a lot of typing with the on-screen keyboard.

Five-Finger Squeeze = Goes to the Home Screen

File finger Squeeze and hold for a moment = Shows App Switcher

Switch between apps. Once you have several apps open and running in full-screen mode, you can switch between them by dragging the little bar at the bottom of the screen to the left or right:

Swipe right or left on the line to switch between running apps.

Cut and Paste Text. To Copy some text, highlight something, and then "pinch" with three fingers to copy text to the clipboard. To paste it, move your cursor elsewhere and expand "or un-pinch" to paste the text back in. If you prefer to Cut the text (copy and delete it), you can simply use the Copy gesture twice. If you have trouble with the various cut/copy/paste gestures, you can alternately tap on the screen with three fingers, which brings up a shortcut menu with those options.

DO NOT DISTURB

Some people find continuously beeping notifications really annoying or distracting when they're trying to get work done. I certainly do. It's also not a good thing to have the iPad beeping and chiming all night while you're trying to sleep. Within the settings app is "Do Not Disturb," where you can silence your iPad in various ways. You can set it to be silent between certain hours, or during "Bedtime." Your Bedtime is a range of times that you can set within the otherwise rarely used Clock App.

From the Control Center (Drag down from the wifi/battery status indicator on the top-right Home Screen), one of the icons is a half-moon. This is the Do Not Disturb control. Do a long-press on the button to get the following screen:

Do Not Disturb Quick Options

Here you can turn off notifications for one hour, until this evening or "Until I leave this location." If you click on "Schedule," it brings up the more advanced setting in the Settings App.

THE MULTIPAD LIFESTYLE

As we have seen, iPads are great for lots of things. What could be better than an iPad? *TWO* iPads!

I'm not suggesting that you run right out and buy two of the things, but Apple's always coming out with new devices, and the new ones always add some great new feature, so the drive to upgrade is very real. Eventually, you're going to want a new model iPad, and rather than try to sell the old one, many people decide hold on to the older one and use both. At the moment, I have the newest model 10.5" iPad Pro, a two-year-old 12.9" iPad Pro, and the most recent iPad Mini. Yes, that makes three of them, but I have to admit, I hardly ever touch the Mini. It's sure handy to have around when I need something ultra-portable though.

I originally planned to use the "big" iPad for work and the smaller 10.5" for games, ebooks, and fun stuff, but that plan didn't last long. I have more-or-less the same apps installed on both, and they stay synced through the cloud. Most of the time, the big iPad sits on my desk with the Smart Keyboard and Pencil, while the 10.5" travels around the house and gets used in places where I don't need the keyboard. The Mini... *sits in the bathroom on a shelf* most of the time, but sometimes goes on overnight trips, as it's easy to pack.

The efficacy of two iPads depends on your usage and the age of the second iPad. The original iPads (model 1, even though they didn't call it that) can still be found on the used market. They still work, although they can't run the latest iOS and may have battery issues. You'd *think* they would be fine for ebooks or photo viewing, but the screen resolution is so low that you probably won't be satisfied after getting used to a newer "retina" screen. Still, you may find a use for even the oldest iPads; they're thick, they're heavy, and they're slow– but most of them **still work**.

If you are looking at getting a cheap used iPad as a spare, I would currently not recommend anything older then the iPad Air or maybe the Air 2. Anything so old that it won't run iOS 11 is going to be just different enough to cause confusion and frustration. It's nice to be able to pick up the closest device and have the apps you need on it, and you can't have that if the old pad won't run the latest stuff.

How you take advantage of a second iPad is up to you; everyone has different needs and processes. Just keep in mind that there's no law limiting you to just a single iPad, and there are many situations and people that call for multiple iPads. You're *not* crazy for wanting two.

Well... maybe a *little* crazy.

CAN YOU DO IT?

Even considering all the apps and procedures we've discussed here, Going iPad isn't for everyone. Sometimes, an app developer just adds more features to the computer version of an app. Some developers don't want to bother with iOS/iPadOS. It's still a growing platform, so if it turns out that "going iPad" isn't going to work for you, don't give up; check back in a few months and see what's developed. If it's not going to work out for you, don't consider the iPad (or yourself) a failure; it's an experiment, not a requirement, right?

Also, I've covered the apps I am most familiar with here. There are almost certainly *entire classes* of software I haven't even thought to include here because I don't use them. Of course, new and better software is released every single day on the App store, and old apps go away as well. It's a constantly-changing, ever-evolving world of software, and you have to be willing to stay on top of things to succeed, especially this year, with the addition of so many new features that make the iPad more computerlike. Software manufacturers will undoubtedly need some time to catch up.

Can you get all your work done using nothing but an iPad?

Probably, but it depends on what you do and how flexible you can be with your workflows. Without any doubt, I can say that switching to an iPad-only lifestyle will be a challenge and require some changes in the way you do things. That said, unless you are locked into some kind of proprietary software or specialized hardware, there's probably some way to do whatever you need to get done.

By accepting the challenge, you gain mobility. You gain simplicity. You gain safety. You gain reliability. You gain the ability to cloud-sync all your work from your phone. There's a lot to be said for all of these benefits, and which one is most important is obviously going to vary from person to person.

THE FUTURE / PREDICTIONS

I really doubt there is going to be much in the way of massive new hardware surprises in the iPad arena for a few years. They'll continue to get faster and thinner, screens will get better, bezels may shrink, batteries will hopefully last longer, but the overall hardware experience probably won't change too much from what we have today. The operating system, on the other hand, has improved tremendously in just the past few years, and there's still plenty of room for future improvement.

Apple's World Wide Developer's Conference (WWDC) is held every summer, and that's when they usually announce and demo the big operating system changes that will be coming. In 2017, they announced iOS 11, which had tremendous improvements in the operating system and multitasking in particular. In 2018's event, they announced iOS 12, which added only a few new features, but big stability and bug fix enhancements. The 2019 event was another major year for the iPad. Apple has historically always worked on a two-year cycle where they introduce a bunch of new features one year, then on the off-year, they work on bug fixes. Will Apple continue this every-other-year cycle now that iPadOS has split off from the iPhone's iOS? Time will tell.

More and more, Apple seems to be centering their offerings around IOS/iPadOS devices, and the Mac seems to slip further into the background every year. It's a slow progression, but it's happening. A few years ago, they announced Project Marzipan, now called Catalyst, that would make it easier for Mac developers to port their apps to the iPad. At the time of this writing, it had only just been released to developers, so nothing has come of it yet, but it seems likely that even more powerful apps will be coming to the iPad soon.

We'll have to see in the next few years how this all turns out. Good luck!

ABOUT THE AUTHOR

I am a former College IT Instructor with an extensive background in computers dating back to the 1980s. Currently, I write on a wide array of topics from computers, to world religions, to ham radio, and I've even released an occasional short horror tale.

I'd love to hear your stories of success and failure with the iPad and getting away from the standard PC world. If there's something you would like to see in a future edition of the book, or otherwise have suggestions, please drop me a note. Contact me at:

Web: http://BrianSchell.com
Email: brian@brianschell.com

Also, please join my email update list— There's NO weekly SPAM or filler material, only announcements of new books or major updates.

Email update link: http://brianschell.com/list/

twitter.com/BrianSchell

facebook.com/Brian.Schell

instagram.com/brian_schell

pinterest.com/brianschell

HOW YOU CAN HELP ME

If you have a suggestion or find a mistake, email me about it, and I'll get it into an updated edition of the book. Got a gripe, complaint, question, or just adoring fan mail? Same thing!

LEAVE A REVIEW

If this book helped you, please leave a review where you purchased this book. Reviews are the best way to help out!

SHARE WITH YOUR FRIENDS

Did you enjoy this book? Please use the buttons below to spread the word to your friends and followers.

ALSO BY BRIAN SCHELL

Amateur Radio

• D-Star for Beginners

• Echolink for Beginners

• DMR for Beginners Using the Tytera MD-380

• SDR for Beginners with the SDRPlay

• Programming Amateur Radios with CHIRP

• FM Satellite Communications for Beginners

• Trunking Scanners for Beginners Using the Uniden TrunkTracker

Technology

• Going Chromebook: Living in the Cloud

• Going Chromebook: Mastering Google Docs

• Going Text: Mastering the Power of the Command Line

• Going iPad: Ditching the Desktop

• DOS Today: Running Vintage MS-DOS Games and Apps on a Modern Computer

Old-Time Radio Listener's Guides

• OTR Listener's Guide to Dark Fantasy

• OTR Listener's Guide to Box 13

The Five-Minute Buddhist Series

• The Five-Minute Buddhist

• The Five-Minute Buddhist Returns

• The Five-Minute Buddhist Meditates

• The Five-Minute Buddhist's Quick Start Guide to Buddhism

• Teaching and Learning in Japan: An English Teacher Abroad

Fiction with Kevin L. Knights:

• Tales to Make You Shiver

• Tales to Make You Shiver 2

• Random Acts of Cloning

• Jess and the Monsters

www.ingramcontent.com/pod-product-compliance
Lightning Source LLC
Chambersburg PA
CBHW070843070326
40690CB00009B/1674